To my dada love - Willa
1st bday!

Quotable Fathers

Milly Brown

summersdale

QUOTABLE FATHERS

Summersdale Publishers Ltd
46 West Street
Chichester
West Sussex
PO19 1RP
UK

www.summersdale.com

Printed and bound by Tien Wah Press, Singapore

All images © Shutterstock

ISBN: 1-84024-668-5
ISBN 13: 978-1-84024-668-1

Quotable Fathers

There is **more** to
fathers than meets
the eye.

Margaret Atwood

It **doesn't matter** who my father was; it matters who I **remember** he was.

Anne Sexton

I wasn't anything **special** as a father. But I **loved them** and they knew it.

Sammy Davis Jr.

There's **no pillow** quite so soft
as a father's **strong** shoulder.

Richard L. Evans

Dad... a son's
first **hero.**

Anonymous

I used to **imagine** animals running under my bed. I told my dad, and he **solved the problem** quickly. He cut the **legs** off the bed.

Lou Brock

It was my father who taught me to **value myself**.

Dawn French

He didn't tell me how to **live**; he lived, and let me **watch** him do it.

Clarence Budington Kelland

You know, **fathers** just have a way of putting everything **together**.

Erika Cosby

Up on his **shoulders**... is where
I love to be.

Michael Carr

Blessed indeed is the man who hears **many gentle voices** call him father!

Lydia M. Child

His **heritage** to his children [was] the **treasure** of his example as a man and a father.

Will Rogers Jr.

When you're a father, you know exactly where **your heart** really is. There's **no question** of it, no doubt.

Fred Ward

On the **beach** at night,
Stands a child with her father,
Watching the east, the **autumn** sky.

Walt Whitman, 'On the Beach at Night'

It's only when you **grow up**...
that you can **measure** his
greatness and fully appreciate it.

Margaret Truman

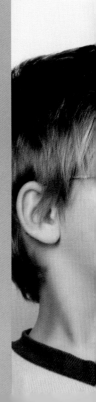

He was **her god**, the centre of her **small** world.

Margaret Mitchell

I am **not ashamed** to say that no man I ever met was my **father's equal**.

Hedy Lamarr

It is a **great moment** in life when a **father sees** a son grow **taller** than he.

Richard L. Evans

A **good** **father** is one of the most unsung, unpraised, **unnoticed**, and yet one of the **most valuable** assets in our society.

Billy Graham

Any **man** can be a father but it takes a **special person** to be a dad.

Anonymous

It's the most **unpredictably wild** thing that ever happened to me. I didn't think **babies** were about that.

Colin Firth

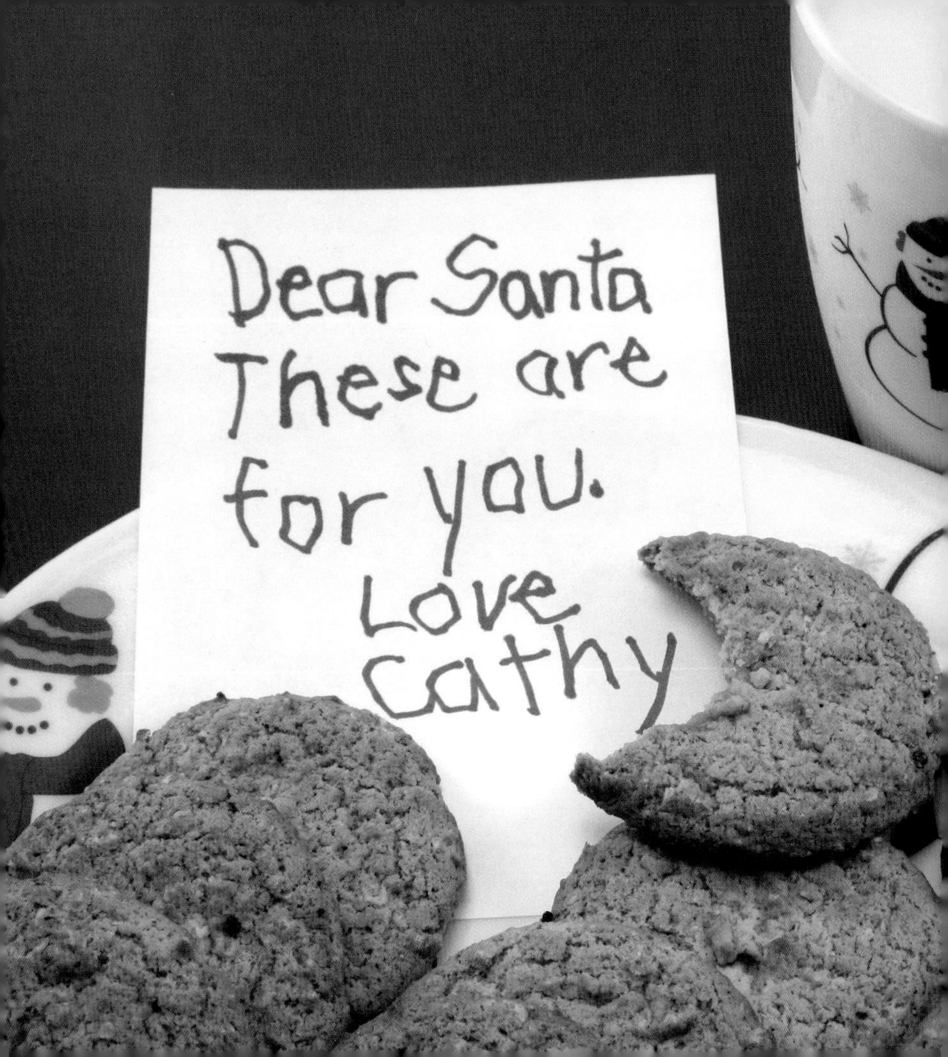
Dear Santa
These are
for you.
Love
Cathy

There are three **stages** of a man's **life**. He believes in **Santa Claus**, he doesn't believe in Santa Claus, he **is** Santa Claus.

Anonymous

How **sweet** 'tis to sit 'neath a **fond** father's **smile**...

John Howard Payne

I **love** my father as the **stars** – he's a bright **shining example** and a happy **twinkling** in my heart.

Adabella Radici

My father was **my teacher**. But most importantly he was a **great** dad.

Beau Bridges

There is a special **place**
in heaven for the father
who takes his **daughter**
shopping.

John Sinor

A truly **rich man** is one whose children run into his **arms** when his **hands are empty**.

Anonymous

... a father who was just **perfect** – never cross, **never unjust**, and always ready for a **game**.

Edith Nesbit, *The Railway Children*

Fatherhood is a very **strange** love and a very **beautiful** love... **unconditional** to the extreme.

Colin Farrell

My father gave me the **greatest gift** anyone could give another person, he **believed** in me.

Jim Valvano

A father is someone you **look up** to, **no matter** how **tall** you are.

Anonymous

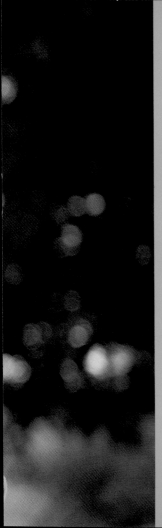

The father **holds** his grown or ungrown son **in his arms** with measureless love...

Walt Whitman, 'The Sleepers'

What we become depends on what our **fathers** teach us at **odd moments**, when they aren't **trying** to teach us.

Umberto Eco

Certain is it that there is no kind of **affection** so purely **angelic** as of a father to a daughter.

Joseph Addison

My father was... **very important** to me, because he made me think.

Janis Joplin

I cannot think of any **need** in **childhood** as strong as the need for a **father's** protection.

Sigmund Freud

To her the **name of father** was another name for **love**.

Fanny Fern

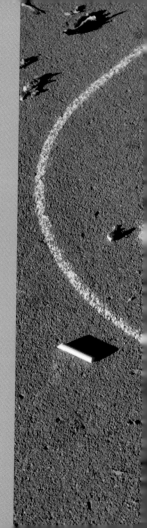

A father is a guy who has **snapshots** in his **wallet** where his **money** used to be.

Anonymous

It is a **wise father** that knows his own child.

William Shakespeare

Old as she was, she still **missed** her **daddy** sometimes.

Gloria Naylor

Safe, for a **child**, is his father's hand, **holding** him tight.

Mario C. Garretty

What's the **most special** thing about being a father? **Everything.**

Viggo Mortensen

My father had a **profound** influence on me, he was a **lunatic**.

Spike Milligan

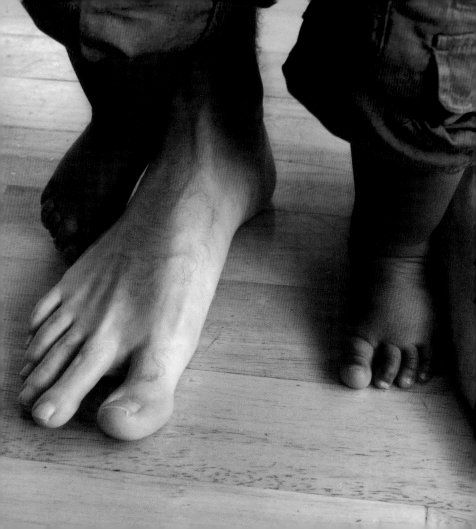

He **follows** his father,
but with **shorter** strides.

Virgil

Why dost **thou weep** in thy gentle sleep?

Awake! thy father does thee keep.

William Blake, 'The Land of Dreams'

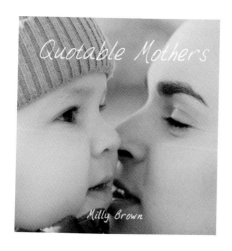

Quotable Mothers

Milly Brown

Hardback

£5.99

ISBN 13: 978 84024 623 0

'Motherhood: all love begins and ends there.'
Robert Browning

This charming collection of poignant quotations and beautiful photographs celebrates the most important women in our lives: our mothers. Whether for Mother's Day, a birthday or just to say thank you for all the great things they do, this book is the perfect way to make any mum feel special.

Quotable Love

Milly Brown

Hardback

£5.99

ISBN 13: 978 84024 663 6

'If I know what love is, it is because of you.'
Herman Hesse

There's no escaping cupid's arrow in this exquisite collection of beautiful, sensual photographs and starry-eyed sayings to warm the hearts of passionate people everywhere.

www.summersdale.com